FOUR VIRUSES WEAKENING THE CHURCH

Chris Fire

© 2016 Chris Fire Ministries, Four Viruses Weakening the Church

All scriptures are quoted from the New King James version unless stated otherwise.

All rights reserved. No portion of this book should be reproduced, stored, distributed, edited, sold, photocopied, or repackaged in any form without prior written permission from the publisher.

ISBN: 978-0692747209

Published by
REVIVAL PUBLISHING

Printed in the United States of America

TABLE OF CONTENTS

Dedication — iv
Preface — v

Part 1: The Virus of Lucifer (Pride)
Chapter 1: What Is the Virus of Lucifer? — 1
Chapter 2: Forms of Pride — 6
Chapter 3: Consequences of Pride — 16

Part 2: The Virus of Delilah (Seduction)
Chapter 4: What Is the Virus of Delilah? — 30
Chapter 5: Things That Attract Delilah — 34
Chapter 6: Her Assignments — 44

Part 3: The Virus of Gehazi (Greed)
Chapter 7: What Is the Virus of Gehazi? — 51
Chapter 8: Types of Greed — 53
Chapter 9: Consequences of Greed — 55

Part 4: The Virus of Jezebel (Witchcraft)
Chapter 10: What Is the Virus of Jezebel? — 65
Chapter 11: Manifestation of the Virus of Jezebel — 67
Chapter 12: Jezebel's Mission — 76

Part 5: Conclusion
Chapter 13: Cures — 85
Chapter 14: Prayer — 89

DEDICATION

I dedicate this book to all Christians who hunger for a fresh outpouring of the Holy Spirit in our generation.
God promised that the glory of the latter rain shall be greater than of the former rain.

Let's keep interceding for all families, churches, communities, cities and nations. For prayer is the only weapon that brings revival and a move of God.

PREFACE

It is with a sense of urgency in my heart, I have written this book because the Holy Spirit has dealt with me concerning this message for so many years. Throughout those years, I have seen the church plagued by sexual immorality, greed, pride, and all types of abominations that have weakened its influence and power on the earth. My humble assignment through this book is to raise our spiritual awareness of the condition of the church. The times are too critical for the church to remain asleep. *Jonah 1:6 (NLT) says, "How can you sleep at a time like this?"*

We can no longer remain asleep while the thief has entered the church and has infiltrated every fiber, from the pulpit to the last person in the pews. The church has fallen so far from a place of integrity, holiness, and righteous that people are no longer coming to church to be saved, changed, and delivered. Rather, they are coming to be entertained. There is no longer a reverence for the presence of God because most of what is identified as the presence of God is merely sensationalism.

We have fed the church an unhealthy spiritual diet for so long that the body of Christ is suffering from spiritual virus and is unable to function at its full potential.

I pray that as you read this book, the Holy Spirit will lay on you the burden to intercede for His church that she will arise to the place of repentance and consecration so that the glory of the latter days can fall on her once again. It's time for the church to eradicate every virus out of her system so she can be stronger again to reach out to the lost and establish the kingdom of God on the earth.

PART 1

The Virus of Lucifer (Pride)

CHAPTER 1
What Is the Virus of Lucifer?

Let me start by saying that there is a difference between feeling proud of an accomplishment and Pride. The dictionary defines pride as "a strong sense of self-respect, a refusal to be humiliated, as well as joy in the accomplishments of oneself or in a person, group, or object that one identifies with." Pride is also used to mean "hubris or excessive pride." This negative connotation of pride is what I call the spirit of Lucifer. Pride (also vanity or arrogance) is "the essentially competitive and excessive belief in one's own abilities that interferes with the individual's recognition of the grace of God or the worth that God sees in others." Pride has been the reason for the fall of many heroes in our society and in the church. It's listed among the six things that God hates in the book of Proverbs.

These six things the LORD hates,
Yes, seven are an abomination to Him:
A proud look, A lying tongue,
Hands that shed innocent blood,
A heart that devises wicked plans,
Feet that are swift in running to evil,
A false witness who speaks lies,
And one who sows discord among brethren.
Proverbs 6:16-19

Four Viruses Weakening The Church
Pride, the First Sin

Isaiah 14:12-15 says: "How you are fallen from heaven, O Lucifer, son of the morning! How you are cut down to the ground, you who weakened the nations! For you have said in your heart: 'I will ascend into heaven, I will exalt my throne above the stars of God; I will also sit on the mount of the congregation on the farthest sides of the north; I will ascend above the heights of the clouds, I will be like the Most High.' Yet you shall be brought down to Sheol, to the lowest depths of the Pit".

You need to understand, beloved, that pride was the first sin to be manifested through Lucifer and to cause a war in the heavens. Rebellion was born because of lucifer's pride. Pride and rebellion always walk hand in hand. Pride manifests itself in the word 'I' because the emphasis is on personal power and not on the grace and the provision from God. Lucifer was created to be a worshipping archangel, giving glory and honor to God forever and ever. However, he began coveting the position of the Most High. People who are prideful usually have a strong desire to be recognized, and they make the point that they are the most high, the most important. A proud person will do anything to be recognized as the most high. One of the main reasons for church splitting is pride. People want to be recognized as the most high; therefore, they rebel against leadership. The sin of pride is not new;

it took place in heaven, and because of that sin, rebellion was born, and one third of the angels were seduced and cast down from heaven.

The Bible calls satan the king of all children of pride, which makes him their father and ruler.

> *"He beholds every high thing;*
> *He is king over all the children of pride" (Job 41:34).*

Whenever you are operating under the spirit of pride, you identify yourself with satan as your father for God is on the side of the humble.

"But He gives more grace. Therefore, He says, 'God opposes the proud, but gives grace to the humble." (James 4:6).

Why Is Pride So Sinful?

I simply define pride as "giving yourself the credit for something that God has accomplished." Pride is appropriating to oneself the glory that belongs to God alone. Pride is essentially self-worship. Anything we accomplish in this world would not have been possible if it were not for God who enables and sustains us. That is why we give God the glory, for He alone deserves it. When you take part in self-worship, what you are saying is simply: "God, I don't need you at all. I can do better by myself, and you are nothing to me."

"But know this, that in the last days, perilous times will come: For men will be lovers of themselves, lovers of money, boasters, proud, blasphemers, disobedient to parents, unthankful, unholy" (2 Timothy 3:1&2).

Pride is one of the signs of the end-time. It's a virus that the enemy is using to keep many people from accepting Jesus Christ as their personal Savior. The refusal to admit sin is a stumbling block for prideful people. Pride keeps a person from acknowledging that in his own strength he cannot do anything to inherit eternal life. You may know that you have offended someone, but pride holds you back from asking for forgiveness. You may realize that you need to reconcile a broken relationship, but pride will lead you to deny that need. The Spirit may convict you of your sinful lifestyle, but pride will discourage you from admitting it. Pride will impede on your service to others. Instead, pride will have you striving for places of prominence. Pride will cause you to listen to flatterers and ignore honest counselors. Pride will lead you to isolate yourself so that you are not accountable to others. We are not to boast about ourselves, but if we want to boast, then we are to proclaim the glory of God. What you say about yourself means nothing in God's work. It is what God says about you that makes the difference.

"But he who glories, let him glory in the LORD.' For not he who commends himself is approved, but whom the Lord commends" (2 Corinthians 10:17&18)

CHAPTER 2
FORMS OF PRIDE

Throughout my studies of the Scriptures, I have discovered two forms of pride that the Bible warns us against: spiritual pride and pride of position. There may be other forms of pride, but I'd like to focus on these two forms because I believe that most believers struggle with them.

Let's analyze them closely.

1. SPIRITUAL PRIDE

In the book of Genesis, we find an interesting conversation in the garden between the serpent and Eve. Satan's strategy was to use the same trick that he had used in heaven when he was cast down. He knew the consequence of Eve's choice would be rebellion. As punishment for the sin of Adam and Eve, God would have to cast them out of the garden, just as He had done in satan's case.

The serpent told Eve that when they ate of the fruit, they would become like God. Let me point out that Adam and Eve had already been created in the image of God; therefore, they were already like God. In other words, they didn't need anything else to make them what they were already. But pride has a way of convincing you that you need additional authority and power to be worth something. I have noticed that most people who struggle with pride also have identity crisis. They are not confident in who they are internally, so they always have to remind everyone of their accomplishments and titles in order to command respect.

Blessed are the poor in spirit,
For theirs is the kingdom of heaven.
Blessed are those who mourn,
For they shall be comforted.
Blessed are the meek,
For they shall inherit the earth. (Matthew 5:3-5)

Let's look at biblical example of spiritual pride.

The Pharisee's Prayer

Luke 18:9-14 shows us an example of spiritual pride in the prayer of the Pharisee in the temple;

"Also He spoke this parable to some who trusted in themselves that they were righteous, and despised others:

"Two men went up to the temple to pray, one a Pharisee and the other a tax collector.

Four Viruses Weakening The Church

The Pharisee stood and prayed thus with himself, 'God, I thank You that I am not like other men—extortioners, unjust, adulterers, or even as this tax collector.
I fast twice a week; I give tithes of all that I possess.'
And the tax collector, standing afar off, would not so much as raise his eyes to heaven, but beat his breast, saying, 'God, be merciful to me a sinner!'

I tell you, this man went down to his house justified rather than the other; for everyone who exalts himself will be humbled, and he who humbles himself will be exalted"

Spiritual pride had blinded this man's heart to his true need of God. He came to the house of God, boasting about his position, his accomplishments, and even his giving. Sometimes we are so proud of the gifts of God in our lives that instead of using our gifts to be a blessing to the body of Christ, we become stumbling blocks. My mentor always said, "We need to be careful how we treat God's people because we are anointed for them."

Spiritual pride has been killing ministries and destinies because it births a competition among us to prove who is better, who is more anointed, or who preaches better, and we wonder why there is division in the body of Christ. Nobody wants to be mentored by or to learn from other ministers. We have become churches of self-made men, always thinking that we are better than the person next to us, the church next to us, and the pastor next to us.

Spiritual pride magnifies the faults of others and diminishes their grace. The spiritually proud man thinks that he has all the answers and therefore neglects knowledge and correction. In most churches today, we don't even take time to lead the people of God to repentance. We start our services with praise and worship, while our hearts are filled with pride. God said in *II Chronicles 7:14*, *"If my people who are called by My name will humble themselves, and pray and seek My face, and turn from their wicked ways, then I will hear from heaven, and will forgive their sin and heal their land."* For the church to experience the move of God, we need to embrace humility in our daily lives.

2. PRIDE OF POSITION

Pharaoh

"Who is the LORD, that I should obey his voice? (Exodus 5:2).

Moses had received the mandate to set the people of Israel free from the captivity of the Egyptians. The Bible says that there was a king who had risen and didn't know anything about Joseph. Apparently, he had never studied the history of the nation he was ruling. During that time, Egypt was the most powerful nation on earth dominating over every level of society. It was the super power of that time, much like the United States is today. Pharaoh thought that he was the ruler of the world, so when Moses came to him to deliver the word of the Lord to set the people of Israel free, Pharaoh refused because of pride.

Man in his pride says the same thing today: Who is God that I should obey His voice? Why should I bow to His authority? Why should I deny myself anything? Why should I ask for help? I don't need God! Oh, what a sin pride is, that it makes you stand up against God and say you will not bow to the authority of God. No matter the position that we attain in this life, God remains the Creator of all and the giver of life.

Naaman

In 2 Kings 5:8-14, we find an interesting story of man called Naaman who was in need of healing.

"So it was, when Elisha the man of God heard that the king of Israel had torn his clothes, that he sent to the king, saying, "Why have you torn your clothes? Please let him come to me, and he shall know that there is a prophet in Israel.

Then Naaman went with his horses and chariot, and he stood at the door of Elisha's house. And Elisha sent a messenger to him, saying, "Go and wash in the Jordan seven times, and your flesh shall be restored to you, and you shall be clean."

But Naaman became furious, and went away and said, "Indeed, I said to myself, 'He will surely come out to me, and stand and call on the name of the LORD his God, and wave his hand over the place, and heal the leprosy.' Are not the Abanah[a] and the Pharpar, the rivers of Damascus, better than all the waters of Israel? Could I not wash in them and be clean?" So he turned and went away in a rage. And his servants came near and spoke to him, and said, "My father, if the prophet had told you to do something great, would you not have done it? How much more then, when he says to you, 'Wash, and be clean'?" So he went down and dipped seven times in the Jordan, according to the saying of the man of God; and his flesh was restored like the flesh of a little child, and he was clean (2 Kings 5:8-14).

We read of the pride of position in Naaman, who almost missed his healing because at first he would not consent to dipping seven times in the Jordan River at the command of the Lord. He was a leper and had gone to God's servant Elisha for healing, but when he heard the terms, he went away in a rage because of his position. He would have returned, still a leper, had a servant of his not talked him into dipping seven times in the Jordan as commanded by the servant of God.

Four Viruses Weakening The Church

Oh, how true this is today: pride of position keeps men from Christ. Men and women everywhere in our society even in the church will not take their place before God as lost sinners because of their positions. Pride of position causes men to perish. Remember: God resist the proud, but gives grace unto the humble. No matter your position in society or what you have accomplished in this life, nothing impresses God because He made you and has the power to unmake you. Before Him, all souls are equal. We need to turn to God so He can give us victory over the sin of pride.

Nebuchadnezzar

All this came upon King Nebuchadnezzar. At the end of the twelve months he was walking about the royal palace of Babylon. The king spoke, saying, "Is not this great Babylon, that I have built for a royal dwelling by my mighty power and for the honor of my majesty?"

While the word was still in the king's mouth, a voice fell from heaven: "King Nebuchadnezzar, to you it is spoken: the kingdom has departed from you! And they shall drive you from men, and your dwelling shall be with the beasts of the field. They shall make you eat grass like oxen; and seven times shall pass over you, until you know that the Most High rules in the kingdom of men, and gives it to whomever He chooses."

That very hour the word was fulfilled concerning Nebuchadnezzar; he was driven from men and ate grass like oxen; his body was wet with the dew of heaven till his hair had grown like eagles' feathers and his nails like birds' claws (Daniel 4:28-33).

We find another example of this pride of position in King Nebuchadnezzar of Babylon. When his heart was lifted up and his mind hardened in pride, he was removed from his kingly throne and his glory was taken from him. Seven long years he roamed the fields and ate grass as an ox. When God got through with him, he could only say: "All the inhabitants of the earth are reputed as nothing: He does according to His will in the army of heaven, and among the inhabitants of the earth. No one can restrain His hand or say to Him, 'What have you done?' and those that walk in pride He is able to put down." What an awful extreme God used to debase this mighty man, break his proud heart, and make him cry for mercy!

Many leaders, both in church and in the secular world, are caught in the trap of the pride of position. I believe that some prominent ministries have failed because of this very same thing. But there is good news! In Daniel 4:34 and 36, we learn that Nebuchadnezzar came back to his senses and acknowledged that God is above all and that there is no one worthy of his glory. God restored him back to power because he humbled himself.

Four Viruses Weakening The Church

Herod

> *So on a set day Herod, arrayed in royal apparel, sat on his throne and gave an oration to them. And the people kept shouting, "The voice of a god and not of a man!" Then immediately an angel of the Lord struck him, because he did not give glory to God. And he was eaten by worms and died.*
> *But the word of God grew and multiplied (Acts 12:21-23).*

If you look closely at this passage, you'll notice that it was the voice of the people that boosted his ego. They compared his voice to that of God. In other words, the people elevated him to the level of God, and God struck him down because he allowed the praise to have an effect on him. Sometimes as leaders, it's easier to become arrogant because of the praise received from the people. I once had a conversation with a preacher who mentioned to me, with a smile of obvious satisfaction that whenever he was absent at his church, the attendance was low. He thought that the response of his congregation was proof of his influence and calling. I had to warn him that pride was getting the best of him. We cannot pay attention to people who praise our talents or abilities to the point where we think that we are irreplaceable. We have to learn to divert all glory to God, not to ourselves.

Chris Fire Ministries

Psalm 115:1 Not to us, O LORD, not to us, but to your name give glory, for your mercy, and for your truth's sake.

CHAPTER 3
Consequences of Pride

The spirit of Lucifer carries consequences in our lives whenever we refuse to deal with it. Sometimes we don't realize that we are under the influence of this virus and that we need to take immediate action until we begin to bear the consequences of it. I'd like to outline a few consequences of this vicious spirit that plagues so many believers and churches, and I pray that God will cause His light to shine on us.

Let's look at the consequences.

1. Pride Casts You Out of the Presence of God.

Moreover, the word of the LORD came to me, saying, "Son of man, take up a lamentation for the king of Tyre, and say to him, 'Thus says the Lord GOD:
"You were the seal of perfection,
Full of wisdom and perfect in beauty.
You were in Eden, the garden of God;
Every precious stone was your covering:
The sardius, topaz, and diamond,
Beryl, onyx, and jasper,
Sapphire, turquoise, and emerald with gold.
The workmanship of your timbrels and pipes
Was prepared for you on the day you were created.

> *"You were the anointed cherub who covers;*
> *I established you;*
> *You were on the holy mountain of God;*
> *You walked back and forth in the midst of fiery stones.*
> *You were perfect in your ways from the day you were created,*
> *Till iniquity was found in you.*
>
> *"By the abundance of your trading*
> *You became filled with violence within,*
> *And you sinned;*
> *Therefore I cast you as a profane thing*
> *Out of the mountain of God;*
> *And I destroyed you, O covering cherub,*
> *From the midst of the fiery stones.*
>
> *"Your heart was lifted up because of your beauty;*
> *You corrupted your wisdom for the sake of your splendor;*
> *I cast you to the ground,*
> *I laid you before kings,*
> *That they might gaze at you'" (Ezekiel 28:11-17).*

The Bible makes it clear that in the beginning Satan was in charge of all the worship in heaven. Satan began to covet God's position and honor because Satan thought that he was better than the Most High. He began to convince other angels that he was better than God, the Creator of heaven and earth.

Whenever people become prideful, they compare themselves to God. One of the characteristics of pride is thinking, "I am self-sufficient and need nobody else, including God."

When Lucifer became prideful in his heart, God deployed the Archangel Michael to evict him from heaven because pride automatically made Lucifer an adversary of God. That is why it is written that God resists the proud. The presence of God symbolizes all of the favor, protection, mercy, and good things that are derived from God. Our pride makes us an automatic enemy of God because we align ourselves with the opposing team. Our pride robs God of His glory.

The virus of pride is one of the reasons our churches today are spiritually dry and bankrupt. We have beautiful buildings, the best instruments, and the finest programs, but there is no power. The presence of God has departed from our churches because of our pride. We began to admire our accomplishments, as if we had done anything by our own strength. We no longer seek God's presence and power because we think that people come to our services because of good preaching and nice buildings.

We need to humble ourselves if we want to see the glory of God return to our churches. The church is not about a man; it's about God. He alone deserves to be the center of attention. David cried out in *Psalm 115:1: "Not unto us, O LORD, not unto us, but unto thy name give glory, for thy mercy, and for thy truth's sake" (KJV)*.

2. Pride Breaks the Prophetic Order.

Then Uzziah prepared for them, for the entire army, shields, spears, helmets, body armor, bows, and slings to cast stones. And he made devices in Jerusalem, invented by skillful men, to be on the towers and the corners, to shoot arrows and large stones. So his fame spread far and wide, for he was marvelously helped till he became strong.

But when he was strong his heart was lifted up, to his destruction, for he transgressed against the LORD his God by entering the temple of the LORD to burn incense on the altar of incense. So Azariah the priest went in after him, and with him were eighty priests of the LORD—valiant men. And they withstood King Uzziah, and said to him, "It is not for you, Uzziah, to burn incense to the LORD, but for the priests, the sons of Aaron, who are consecrated to burn incense. Get out of the sanctuary, for you have trespassed! You shall have no honor from the LORD God."

Then Uzziah became furious; and he had a censer in his hand to burn incense. And while he was angry with the priests, leprosy broke out on his forehead, before the priests in the house of the LORD, beside the incense altar.

Four Viruses Weakening The Church

(2 Chronicles 26:14-19).

Here we see a typical result of pride. The Bible makes it clear that Uzziah prospered because he sought The Lord in the days of Zechariah, who had understanding of visions.

Uzziah did accomplish great things for God and his people, but because of pride, he dared to enter the temple to burn incense. According to the tradition of Israel, priests were the only ones responsible for burning incense on the altar. The priest and the prophet were responsible to anoint a person as king by divine direction. God was setting the pattern of order by establishing the authority of the church and then the government. That's why I believe that the church should never take orders from the government, but the nation must look up to the church for the prosperity of the land.

Uzziah said to himself, "After all, I am the king over Israel; I have been anointed and have authority. Why should I always wait for a priest to offer sacrifice for me? I can do it on my own." His pride set the stage to break the prophetic order established by God. As a result, God struck him down with leprosy. Isn't it interesting that even in the church, people do things that they were never anointed for, just because of pride? I have learned something in life: no matter how old people get and how much they accomplish in life, their parents and spiritual fathers are still in the place of authority before God.

I also strongly believe that pride is one of the root cause of rebellion. We think that we can do a better job than our pastors, managers, or bosses, and we begin to discredit the leader in our own favor. Pride is The reason why people break away from churches. Pride brings a spirit of competition. We must be very careful that at every level of our life we don't attract a curse over us because of pride.

3. Pride Brings the Judgment of God.

Now Satan stood up against Israel, and moved David to number Israel. So David said to Joab and to the leaders of the people, "Go, number Israel from Beersheba to Dan, and bring the number of them to me that I may know it."

And Joab answered, "May the LORD make His people a hundred times more than they are. But, my lord the king, are they not all my lord's servants? Why then does my lord require this thing? Why should he be a cause of guilt in Israel?"

Nevertheless, the king's word prevailed against Joab. Therefore Joab departed and went throughout all Israel and came to Jerusalem. Then Joab gave the sum of the number of the people to David. All Israel had one million

Four Viruses Weakening The Church

one hundred thousand men who drew the sword, and Judah had four hundred and seventy thousand men who drew the sword. But he did not count Levi and Benjamin among them, for the king's word was abominable to Joab.

And God was displeased with this thing; therefore, He struck Israel. So David said to God, "I have sinned greatly, because I have done this thing; but now, I pray, take away the iniquity of your servant, for I have done very foolishly."

Then the LORD spoke to Gad, David's seer, saying, "Go and tell David, saying, 'Thus says the LORD: 'I offer you three things; choose one of them for yourself, that I may do it to you.'"

So Gad came to David and said to him, "Thus says the LORD: 'Choose for yourself, either three[a] years of famine, or three months to be defeated by your foes with the sword of your enemies overtaking you, or else for three days the sword of the LORD—the plague in the land, with the angel[b] of the LORD destroying throughout all the territory of Israel.' Now consider what answer I should take back to Him who sent me."

And David said to Gad, "I am in great distress. Please let me fall into the hand of the LORD, for His mercies are very great; but do not let me fall into the hand of man."

So the LORD sent a plague upon Israel, and seventy thousand men of Israel fell.

And God sent an angel to Jerusalem to destroy it. As he[c] was destroying, the LORD looked and relented of the disaster, and said to the angel who was destroying, "It is enough; now restrain your[d] hand." And the angel of the LORD stood by the threshing floor of Ornan[e] the Jebusite.

Then David lifted his eyes and saw the angel of the LORD standing between earth and heaven, having in his hand a drawn sword stretched out over Jerusalem. So David and the elders, clothed in sackcloth, fell on their faces.

And David said to God, "Was it not I who commanded the people to be numbered? I am the one who has sinned and done evil indeed; but these sheep, what have they done? Let Your hand, I pray, O LORD my God, be against me and my father's house, but not against Your people that they should be plagued (1 Chronicles 21:1-17).

This Scriptural story has an interesting introduction. We learn that Satan himself tempted David. It's among the few instances in the Old Testament where the name of Satan appears. The Bible says that Satan (the spirit of Lucifer) influenced David into numbering his people. In those days in Israel, the census of the population was only

Four Viruses Weakening The Church

supposed to be done before heading to war or for taxes purposes. But David decided to number the people Israel to admire the strength and power of his kingdom. God was displeased with David because pride was the main motivation in his decision. The Scriptures make it clear that God dispatched an angel of death that slew the men of Israel. These men had done nothing wrong, but because the leader was prideful, God began to destroy the source of David's pride. God said, "David, remember where I took you from, how I gave you victory over Goliath with a stone, how I protected you from Saul, and how I caused nations to submit to you. Even when nobody believed in you, I had faith in you and made you who you are. Now you want to put me aside and number the people. And by doing so, you are saying that you succeeded not because of Me but because of your troops?"

How true is it in our lives, we often at times become so prideful that we begin to put our trust in things that God has blessed us with, and thus forfeit His position of trust in our lives. In the same manner that God in the old testament began to kill the people, He will kill the very thing in which we place our trust and about which we boast. We bring God's judgment upon ourselves whenever we operate under the spirit of pride.

4. *Pride Despises the Grace of God*

And many brought gifts to the LORD at Jerusalem, and presents to Hezekiah king of Judah, so that he was exalted in the sight of all nations thereafter.
In those days Hezekiah was sick and near death, and he prayed to the LORD; and He spoke to him and gave him a sign. But Hezekiah did not repay according to the favor shown him, for his heart was lifted up; therefore, wrath was looming over him and over Judah and Jerusalem.
(2 Chronicles 32:23-25).

This virus of pride is illogical because all that we possess is from God. He alone gives us health, wealth, strength, wisdom, and the ability to work, plan and labor at our job. He alone gives us everything we have. Without Him, we can do nothing–absolutely nothing; we are the creations of His hands, and we did not make ourselves.

God, in His sovereignty, has placed us into the family and nation into which we were born; He chose our skin color, environment, and all the details that make up our lives. We receive nothing, spiritually or physically, except it comes to us from above; therefore, what do we have to be proud of? If we have received anything in this life, it has come from God!

Hezekiah was sick and near death, so he prayed to God for healing, and God healed him. When he did get well, he did not show any gratitude to God because his heart was prideful. He despised the grace of God.

> *12 At that time Berodach-Baladan[a] the son of Baladan, king of Babylon, sent letters and a present to Hezekiah, for he heard that Hezekiah had been sick. 13 And Hezekiah was attentive to them, and showed them all the house of his treasures—the silver and gold, the spices and precious ointment, and all[b] his armory—all that was found among his treasures. There was nothing in his house or in all his dominion that Hezekiah did not show them.*
>
> *14 Then Isaiah the prophet went to King Hezekiah, and said to him, "What did these men say, and from where did they come to you?"*
>
> *So Hezekiah said, "They came from a far country, from Babylon."*
>
> *15 And he said, "What have they seen in your house?"*
>
> *So Hezekiah answered, "They have seen all that is in my house; there is nothing among my treasures that I have not shown them."*
>
> *16 Then Isaiah said to Hezekiah, "Hear the word of the LORD: 17 'Behold, the days are coming when all that is in your house, and what your fathers have accumulated until this day, shall be carried to Babylon; nothing shall be left,' says the LORD. 18 'And they shall take away some of your sons who will descend from you, whom you will beget; and they shall be eunuchs in the palace of the king of Babylon.'*
> *(2 kings 20:12-18)*

Again we read the following verses of admonition in

Psalm 75:4-7.
I said to the boastful, 'Do not deal boastfully,'
And to the wicked, 'Do not lift up the horn.
Do not lift up your horn on high;
Do not speak with a stiff neck.'
For exaltation comes neither from the east
Nor from the west nor from the south.
But God is the Judge: He puts down one, And exalts another.

Let's Reason

If we are saved, it is only by God's sovereign grace, if we have any good thing, it has been given to us from above! If we have any gift, it was given to us by the Holy Spirit Who gives to every man as He pleases. He does it in a sovereign way. If we are able to work out our own salvation with fear and trembling, it is because the Holy Spirit works in us to will and to do according to His good pleasure. If our eyes have been enlightened to see and receive any spiritual truth, it is because the Holy Spirit taught us and opened the Word to us. If we are able to do a good work for God, it is because of His sufficiency.

"Not that we are sufficient of ourselves to think of anything as being from ourselves, but our sufficiency is from God" (2 Corinthians 3:5).

Four Viruses Weakening The Church

It is because of God's mercies that we are not consumed. It is because of God's love that we have been drawn to Him. It is because of His everlasting arms under us that we are kept. It is by faith in Him that we are saved; by His blood we are cleansed; by His righteousness we are clothed; by His power we are kept; by His grace we are sustained; by His intercession we are delivered; by His Indwelling Spirit we are filled; and by His goodness we are led to repentance. All that God has for His people is from the Father, through the Son, and by the Holy Spirit.

Therefore, what do we have to be proud of? Nothing, for all has been given to us from above. So let us bow at the footstool of Christ; let us pour out our hearts in confession of this sin of pride. Let us seek His face in forgiveness and forever hide in Christ, for He is our safe hiding place and we are complete in Him.

Now these things, brethren, I have figuratively transferred to myself and Apollos for your sakes, that you may learn in us not to think beyond what is written, that none of you may be puffed up on behalf of one against the other. For who makes you differ from another? And what do you have that you did not receive? Now if you did indeed receive it, why do you boast as if you had not received it?
(1 Corinthians 4:6-7)

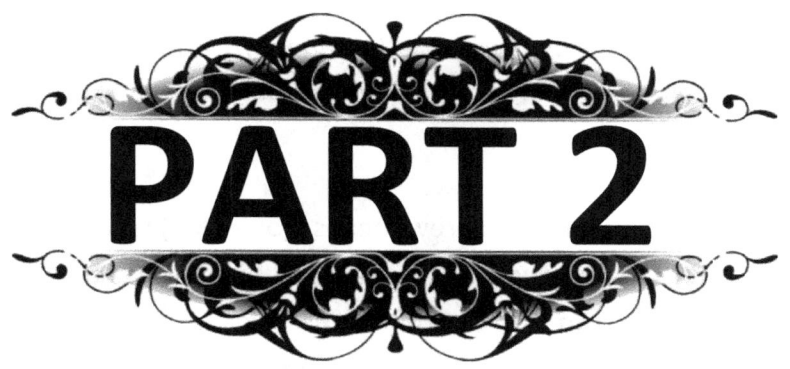

The Virus of Delilah
(Seduction)

CHAPTER 4
What Is the Virus of Delilah?

Delilah was well-known in the Bible as a woman who succeeded in unlocking the secret of Samson's strength.

"Afterward it happened that he [Samson] loved a woman in the Valley of Sorek, whose name was Delilah" (Judges 16:4).

The word Delilah in Hebrew means "(one who) weakened, uprooted or impoverished." We need to understand that people don't do things just for the sake of doing them; there is always a spirit element or an influence that leads people to do right or wrong.

When we talk about the virus of Delilah, we are not referring to the person of Delilah but rather to the unseen element that was operating in her life. The spirit of Delilah has been in operation for centuries in different forms and at different levels, but always with the same goal—to weaken our vision and uproot us from our destinies. Most Christians think that the spirit of Delilah only affects women, but this is not true, men are also influenced by this same spirit.

The spirit of Delilah is a virus that the enemy has unleashed on every front in this end time. This spirit is a master spirit that includes seduction, fornication, adultery, pornography, masturbation, and similar practices. But I also want to broaden your understanding about this spirit. Even though it manifests itself in sexual seduction, this spirit includes any form of seduction that weakens your vision, uproots you from your destiny, and impoverishes your life. The enemy has targeted the body of Christ in this end time and injected this virus into the church. Being a Christian doesn't automatically shield you against this spirit. It's obedience and submission to the Word of the Lord, along with intense discipline that will help you to stand.

Let me give two examples to reinforce the fact that the anointing or the calling of God over your life doesn't automatically give you victory over this virus. Samson, the strongest man who ever lived, was able to carry the gates of the city on his shoulders, kill a lion with his bare hands, and destroy an army all by himself. One person who had been able to work wonders by the power of Jehovah ended up losing a battle against this virus. Another example of a mighty man is David, a king called and anointed by God, who was so skilled in battles that his enemies were greatly afraid of Him. He was still anointed that day when he stood in his palace and coveted Bathsheba and eventually fell into fornication.

The church in Corinth was characterized by strong demonstrations of the gifts of the spirit, yet they were so carnal and plagued with immorality that Paul told them to

Four Viruses Weakening The Church

flee from sexual immorality. Another word of advice to remember is that the only way you can have victory over this spirit is to run away from it. Never put yourself in a situation or an environment that is conducive to the virus of Delilah.

"Flee from sexual immorality. All other sins a person commits are outside the body, but whoever sins sexually, sins against their own body" (I Corinthians 6:18 NIV).

Chris Fire Ministries

CHAPTER 5
Things That Attract Delilah

In order for us to protect ourselves against this virus that is crippling to the church, it's important to understand the environment in which it operates and the conditions that cause it to flourish.

1. Loneliness

Loneliness is a mental state of isolation. Samson dealt with loneliness in his life. The Bible says that he was first married to a Philistine woman who was killed with her family because Samson asked for a riddle that the Philistines could not interpret. This resulted in Samson having to carry on by himself despite of the loneliness in his heart and soul. Samson no longer had a companion.

Samson was anointed but lonely. When the Philistines wanted to set him up to be captured, they chose Delilah, a Philistine woman like the wife he had lost. There is no record in the Bible that Samson ever organized a troop of men to fight the Philistines. He was a lonely soldier, a lonely leader, a lonely visionary, and a lonely man.

I have counseled many married men and women. You would be amazed how many of them feel lonely even though they are married. They feel empty on the inside because they feel something is missing. Onetime, we were praying for a sister who admitted that even while she was married, she had lusted for her coworker because she felt that he made her feel special and offered her all of the caring and attention that she was not getting from her husband. The result was that she ended up having an affair within a year.

You must understand that the enemy always likes to separate us from other believers and put us in a tight corner by ourselves so he can have the advantage over us. In reference to friendship, the Bible says "iron sharpens iron." The work of the kingdom cannot be done alone; we need like-minded men and women who can pray and fast with us and to whom we are accountable. No soldier wants to be by himself on the battlefield. Being alone makes a person more vulnerable to the enemy. Every Christian must be a part of a local church where he or she is fed the true Word of God, which is able to build them up and give them an inheritance in Christ Jesus.

Two are better than one,
Because they have a good reward for their labor.
For if they fall, one will lift up his companion.
But woe to him who is alone when he falls,
For he has no one to help him up.
Again, if two lie down together, they will keep warm;
But how can one be warm alone?
Though one may be overpowered by another, two can withstand him.

Four Viruses Weakening The Church

And a threefold cord is not quickly broken (Ecclesiastes 4:9-12).

There is power in unity. We are more powerful and dangerous to the kingdom of the enemy when we walk united. The principle of unity is critical to the success of your mission and strengthens your purpose in every level of life. No wonder that one of the enemy's agendas is to divide the body of Christ so he can isolate the people of God from each other. You will always want to network with people who will help you advance in life.

2. Distraction

Distraction is defined as "the diverting of the attention of an individual or group from the chosen object of attention onto the source of distraction." Distraction is caused by one of the following: lack of ability to pay attention; lack of interest in the object of attention; greater interest in something other than the object of attention; or the great intensity or attractiveness of the source of distraction. Distractions can come from people, situations, or even from your own self.

"And this I say for your own profit, not that I may put a leash on you, but for what is proper, and that you may serve the Lord without distraction" (1 Corinthians 7:35).

Samson, whose mission was to liberate the people of Israel from the Philistines, went to Gaza and ended up with a harlot because he became distracted by things other than his assignment. Distractions can sidetrack you and therefore cause you to be in places where you had no businesses being or to become involved in activities that offer no spiritual reward. In this technological generation, the spirit of Delilah is closer than we think. The enemy has placed his seductive devices all over the place to allure us into his snares.

Distraction is one of the greatest tools that Satan is using in the end times because distraction has the ability to kill your discipline and focus. It can also lead to procrastination, which causes delays in fulfilling tasks or responsibilities. Many people miss out on life because they are easily sidetracked by so many things that don't move them forward. Time is a perishable gift that can never be recovered once it's lost, so you need to make the most of your time by avoiding any distractions in your life.

3. *Prayerlessness*

I read the story of Samson for many years and never noticed the following aspect of his life: prayerlessness. Only two instances in the Bible mention that Samson prayed. First he prayed the following: *"Then he became very thirsty; so he cried out to the LORD and said, "You have given this great deliverance by the hand of Your servant; and now shall I die of thirst and fall into the hand of the uncircumcised?" (Judges 15:18)*. And again after he fell under the virus of Delilah, he prayed: *"Then Samson called to the LORD, saying, 'O Lord GOD, remember me, I pray! Strengthen me, I pray, just this once, O God, that I may with one blow take vengeance on the Philistines for my two eyes!'" (Judges 16:28)*.

Samson's prayers were very self-centered. He prayed because he was thirsty, and then he prayed so he could avenge the loss of his two eyes. There was no pattern of consistent prayer for grace and power to fulfill his mission and mandate.

The virus of prayerlessness is crippling the church. Believers are not connecting to God the way they should. Like Samson, we pray when we face challenges and difficulties in our lives—emergency prayers. Prayer should be a relationship with God, not a fix-my-problem system. That is why most of us are still facing challenges. We were anointed at one point, yet we are still carnal. Why? Because the anointing, or the presence, of God is not permanently with us. As I studied the life of Samson, one thing I realized is that the Spirit of God came upon Him to enable him to fulfill an assignment, but once he had finished the task, the spirit departed from Him.

Prayer is the element that guarantees the permanent presence of God. We need the abiding presence and awesomeness of God in our lives. Many Christians are spiritually weak because they don't pray.

God called and anointed Samson, but it was Samson's responsibility to guard that anointing through consecration by prayer. Whatever is birthed in prayer must be maintained by prayer. My spiritual father, the Archbishop N. Duncan-Williams, wrote a book entitled *The Supernatural Power of a Praying Man*. The book contains an in depth the virus of prayerlessness and how to overcome it. I highly recommend this book as a powerful tool to impact your prayer life.

4. Disobedience

It happened in the spring of the year, at the time when kings go out to battle, that David sent Joab and his servants with him, and all Israel; and they destroyed the people of Ammon and besieged Rabbah. But David remained at Jerusalem.

Then it happened one evening that David arose from his bed and walked on the roof of the king's house. And from the roof he saw a woman bathing, and the woman was very beautiful to behold. So David sent and inquired about the woman. And someone said, "Is this not Bathsheba, the daughter of Eliam, the wife of Uriah the Hittite?" Then David sent messengers, and took her; and she came to him, and he lay with her, for she was cleansed from her impurity; and she returned to her house (2 Samuel 11:1-4).

Four Viruses Weakening The Church

David was supposed to go to war with all his mighty warriors. He was the leader of Israel and the commander in chief. The Bible makes it clear that this was the time when the kings went out to battle. Instead, David chose to remain in Jerusalem and not to fight. David had positioned himself to be ensnared by the spirit of seduction. He disobeyed the law and found himself in a place of laziness—distraction. By disobedience, the spirit of seduction found its way in and led David down a path that led to murder. John 5:17 says that even Jesus was busy working, *"But Jesus answered them, "My Father has been working until now, and I have been working."*

We must understand that this is a time of war, and every believer should put on the full armor of God to be able to withstand the evil days. It troubles me when I see church prayer and intercession meetings where there is no pastor or leader present. It would be understandable if these leaders were on prophetic assignments, but sometimes that is not the case. The same goes for every Christian. When the pastor calls for a prayer meeting at the church, some believers don't attend, they rather stay at home and watch TV or browse the internet. Whenever a person disobeys God's Word, he puts himself in a place of great vulnerability.

5. **Self Credit**

So Delilah said to Samson, "Please tell me where your great strength lies, and with what you may be bound to afflict you."

And Samson said to her, "If they bind me with seven fresh bowstrings, not yet dried, then I shall become weak, and be like any other man."

So the lords of the Philistines brought up to her seven fresh bowstrings, not yet dried, and she bound him with them. Now men were lying in wait, staying with her in the room. And she said to him, "The Philistines are upon you, Samson!" But he broke the bowstrings as a strand of yarn breaks when it touches fire. So the secret of his strength was not known.

Then Delilah said to Samson, "Look, you have mocked me and told me lies. Now, please tell me what you may be bound with."

So he said to her, "If they bind me securely with new ropes that have never been used, then I shall become weak, and be like any other man."

Therefore, Delilah took new ropes and bound him with them, and said to him, "The Philistines are upon you, Samson!" And men were lying in wait, staying in the room. But he broke them off his arms like a thread.

Delilah said to Samson, "Until now you have mocked me and told me lies. Tell me what you may be bound with."

And he said to her, "If you weave the seven locks of my head into the web of the loom"—

Four Viruses Weakening The Church

So she wove it tightly with the batten of the loom, and said to him, "The Philistines are upon you, Samson!" But he awoke from his sleep, and pulled out the batten and the web from the loom.

Then she said to him, "How can you say, 'I love you,' when your heart is not with me? You have mocked me these three times, and have not told me where your great strength lies." And it came to pass, when she pestered him daily with her words and pressed him, so that his soul was vexed to death, that he told her all his heart, and said to her, "No razor has ever come upon my head, for I have been a Nazirite to God from my mother's womb. If I am shaven, then my strength will leave me, and I shall become weak, and be like any other man."

When Delilah saw that he had told her all his heart, she sent and called for the lords of the Philistines, saying, "Come up once more, for he has told me all his heart." So the lords of the Philistines came up to her and brought the money in their hand. Then she lulled him to sleep on her knees, and called for a man and had him shave off the seven locks of his head. Then she began to torment him, and his strength left him. (Judges16:6-18).

Samson gave credit to himself by saying that his strength was in his hair. The truth was that his strength was in God because without God he could not have done the things that he did. The hair was a sign of a covenant, but his hair did not possess the power that enabled him to have victory over the Philistines. Isn't it true that most of the time, we consider the resources that God has given us as the source? Let me explain it this way: your job can put a roof over your head, but your job in itself is not a source; God is using it to bless you. Your job is a resource in God's hands, yet God remains the source of not only your job but all things. When we give credit to our resources and boast in them, we anger God because the Bible says in *Isaiah 42:8, "I am the LORD, that is my name; and My glory I will not give to another, Nor My praise to carved images."*

We need to learn to always give God glory in our lives. Sometimes we give credit to everything but God. We credit our education, our parents, or our friends, but we fail to honor the ultimate One from whom all things come. Every time you credit your strength and blessings to anything but God, what you are literally doing is removing God from the picture and negating His grace upon your life.

CHAPTER 6
Her Assignments

1. *To kill the mighty Men*

The Enemy knows that as long as there is a leader walking according to the counsel of God, he is in trouble. A mighty man is the one who assures stability and peace for his territory. The Devil will try to kill him by injecting a virus called the spirit of Delilah. When I use the phrase mighty men, it's simply to refer to those who have a mission and destiny from God. This includes both men and women.

God consecrated Samson to be judge over Israel and to set the people of God free from the persecution of their enemies, the Philistines. Samson had a record of courting women that he had no business being with. He married a Philistine woman, had a one-night stand with a prostitute, and since the virus of Delilah was not treated, it slowly developed to infect every part of him and eventually weaken his spiritual body. It is sad to say, but many churches have suffered from this virus and lost their leaders, pastors, head ministry leader, deacons, elders, and even members.

Not only churches, but a lot of families have suffered because of this virus. Marriages have been destroyed, and lives have been lost. This virus kills your purpose and destiny. It can alter your destiny and bring you to the place of the death of your purpose, calling, and dreams. Because of this virus, there are men of God whose reputations are destroyed and politicians who can no longer hold a position of public trust. This virus of seduction and lust has birthed numerous marital affairs making divorce rampant in society.

In the midst of such widespread lust, there is good news; the Bible says that the lamb was slain before the foundation of the earth. God has the power to bring you back to life; He can resurrect your purpose, your destiny, and your calling if you are willing to repent and ask God for deliverance.

2. Abort Your Assignment

Your assignment is more valuable and important than anything life can offer. It is the very reason why you are still on this earth. When your mission is aborted, it literally means that you have no reason to remain on earth. You become useless. The desire of satan is to bring you to the point where you are useless to your family, to the house of God, and to the kingdom of God. This has caused many people to come short of their calling. The Devil is after you because of the assignment of your life. I often say that the Devil doesn't waste time with people who don't go anywhere. He is too busy to afford that luxury. He targets those who have both purpose and dream. Because of Moses' assignment, Pharaoh killed all of the firstborn of Israel to prevent the deliverer from arising. Joseph fled with his family to Egypt because Herod wanted to destroy the assignment on Jesus' life.

The first thing that the enemy does to abort your assignment is to kill your vision. Your vision allows you able to reach and fulfill your assignment. Vision is the ability to see where you are going. The first thing that the Philistines did when they finally captured Samson was to gouge out his eyes because without vision, the people perish.

"Then the Philistines seized him, gouged out his eyes and took him down to Gaza. Binding him with bronze shackles, they set him to grinding grain in the prison"
(Judges 16:21 NIV).

3. Pressure You

Then she said to him, "How can you say, 'I love you,' when your heart is not with me? You have mocked me these three times, and have not told me where your great strength lies." And it came to pass, when she pestered him daily with her words and pressed him, so that his soul was vexed to death, that he told her all his heart, and said to her, "No razor has ever come upon my head, for I have been a Nazirite to God from my mother's womb. If I am shaven, then my strength will leave me, and I shall become weak, and be like any other man (Judges16: 15-17).

Delilah insisted that Samson reveal his secret to her. Three times she asked Samson to do so, and she employed every strategy that she thought could get her that result. Samson was troubled by her comments, and her consistent pressure caused him to give in to her deceit. The Devil also works by applying pressure. It's critical to know your enemy's tactics in order for you to put up a better defense. In II Corinthians 2:11, Paul tells us not to be ignorant of Satan's devices, lest he gain advantage over us. The battle begins in our mind. The Enemy and his demons will apply pressure to your thoughts and habits to make you break and eventually give in. They will try to saturate your mind with thoughts of viewing pornography in various forms, flirting with idea of having an affair, or fantasizing about sleeping with another person who is not your partner. These types of thoughts are usually derived from the internet, television or conversations with the wrong people. We must put up a strong defense to guard our mind—for out of it comes the issues of life.

We need to allow our minds to think on those things that are worthy. This means that it's within our ability to fight any negative thought and pressure from the enemy. Don't feed your mind on the pressure of the enemy; rather, shift your mind to think on the things above. *"Finally, brothers and sisters, whatever is true, whatever is noble, whatever is right, whatever is pure, whatever is lovely, whatever is admirable--if anything is*

Four Viruses Weakening The Church

excellent or praiseworthy--think about such things"
(Philippians 4:8 NIV).

4. To cause God's presence to depart from you

Samson slept with Delilah after telling her his secret. The Bible makes it clear that when Delilah shouted that the Philistines were there, Samson rose up and proceeded to attack them as he usually had done. But now it was different. The Spirit of the Lord had departed from him, and he knew it not. It's a terrible thing to try to do the work of God without God's presence. When His Spirit departs from you, you become vulnerable to the enemy.

"And she said, 'The Philistines are upon you, Samson!' So he awoke from his sleep, and said, 'I will go out as before, at other times, and shake myself free!' But he did not know that the LORD had departed from him" (Judges 16:20).

When David sinned against God with Beersheba by falling into this virus of the enemy, God sent the prophet Nathan to bring his servant into alignment. Since David knew and understood that the virus he was infected with causes the spirit of God to depart, David acknowledged and repented before God and said, "Don't take away thy spirit from me." Sexual immorality is one of the sins that involve your body, your soul, and your spirit, and it automatically leaves no room for the Holy Ghost to reside in.

However, it's possible to perform the work of God without the God of the work, and many people are deceived when they fall prey to the spirit of Delilah. They think that as long as they can preach, sing, or serve, God's presence must still be with them. Jesus said in Matthew 7:22-23, *"Many will say to me on that day, 'Lord, Lord, did we not prophesy in your name, and in your name cast out demons, and in your name perform many miracles?' And then I will declare to them, 'I never knew you; DEPART FROM ME, YOU WHO PRACTICE LAWLESSNESS.'"*

CHAPTER 6

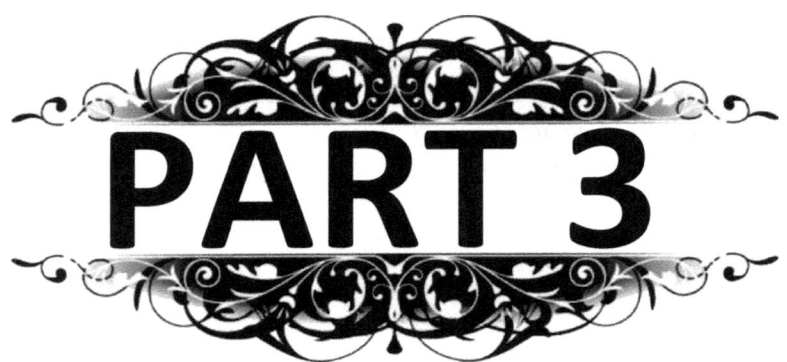

The Virus of Gehazi (Greed)

CHAPTER 7
What Is the Virus of Gehazi?

The virus of Gehazi is one of the deadliest spiritual viruses to affect humanity. It refers to the spirit of greed that is crippling both the church and our society at every level. Greed is defined as "an excessive desire to acquire or possess more [especially more material wealth] than one needs or deserves." Avarice is defined as "reprehensible acquisitiveness; insatiable desire for wealth." A reasonable desire to increase one's wealth is nearly universal and acceptable in any culture, and this simple want is not considered greed. Greed is the extreme form of this desire, especially where one desires things simply for the sake of owning them. Greed may entail acquiring material possessions at the expense of another's welfare.

I define greed as simply "a selfish desire to possess more than you will ever need." The Bible refers to greed as "covetousness; selfish ambition." Unfortunately, today, our society has taught us that greed is good for both business and individuals because it is the source of motivation... But let me tell you, that is a big lie from the Enemy. Jesus knew the deadly danger of greed and warned his disciples to be careful: *"Then he said to them, 'Watch out! Be on your guard against all kinds of greed; life does not consist in the abundance of his possessions'"* (*Luke 12:15 NIV*).

Four Viruses Weakening The Church

The reason why greed takes place in our lives is that we have the wrong view of life. The world system makes us believe that the more possessions we have, the more enjoyable and peaceful life will be; the more money we have, the more stress-free we will be. I've seen and heard of people with an abundance of money who are depressed and even commit suicide. Jesus, knowing the source of greed, told his disciples to adjust their view of life. He told them that life doesn't consist of the abundance of possessions. The spirit of greed has destroyed numerous families, relationships, churches, and organizations. It is a poison that starts inside someone's heart and soon affects all his surroundings. Today the great commission is suffering because of the greed of some people. The greed of people occupying places of influence and authority in governments and institutions has caused a lot of people to suffer. Greed is not a goal—for there is no end to it. No matter how much the greedy possess, they want more. The spirit of greed can result in corruption, murder, hatred, lies and disgrace. Greed is a condition of the heart that only God can change through the power of His Word.

CHAPTER 8
Types of Greed

Jesus warned his disciples about all varieties of greed. *"Watch out! Be on your guard against all kinds of greed; a man's life does not consist in the abundance of his possessions" (Luke 12:15 NIV).* He advises us of the different types of greed.

Notice the following two forms of greed:

1. **Greed for Power**

This type of greed is affecting the church in many different forms and shape. It causes believers in the church to become more focused on titles and positions. It is sad to see that in the church, people fight for position and even attack each other's character. Satan is fulfilling his mission because he has succeeded in infusing a spirit of greed in believers to hinder the progress of the gospel. People who are greedy for power usually do not understand the role and responsibility of authority. When God gave authority and dominion to Adam, it was in order for him to make this earth a better place.

Today people are seeking power for their own ego and agenda, thus giving the enemy an access point to frustrate, attack, and scatter the people of God. Many churches have suffered division in their midst because believers didn't want to submit to authority or leadership.

Four Viruses Weakening The Church

People are leaving churches just because the pastors did not recognize their contribution to a particular ministry. Please understand that men can only reward you with earthly things, but God can give you eternal rewards. So whether a pastor recognizes me or not, it should not matter as long as I know that this is where God has placed me to fulfill my calling.

One of the dangers of this form of greed is that it can expose you prematurely to power, money, and influence. Have you heard the phrase "Leaders are made and not born"? What it simply means is that becoming a leader is a process. The Bible says God called Jacob, and He made Israel. Israel was the name that Jacob received after wrestling with the angel of God. He went through a process to become Israel. The greed for power makes you believe that you don't need the training or processing time to move from one level to the next. I have seen people in the corporate world who were ready to do anything to move up in rank or position. We must understand that it is God Who gives us all things. What God has planned for you, he will make available to you at the appropriate time and season.

2. **Greed for Acquisition**

This form of greed brings a strong desire for accumulation—wanting too much of something or being afraid that you'll run out of something; therefore, you desire more. One of my friends told me a story about a rich woman who kept her money under her bed because she was afraid of losing it. This type of greed is often related to finances.

Then He spoke a parable to them, saying: "The ground of a certain rich man yielded plentifully. And he thought within himself, saying, 'What shall I do, since I have no room to store my crops?' So he said, 'I will do this: I will pull down my barns and build greater, and there I will store all my crops and my goods. And I will say to my soul, "Soul, you have many goods laid up for many years; take your ease; eat, drink, and be merry."' But God said to him, 'Fool! This night your soul will be required of you; then whose will those things be which you have provided?'
"So is he who lays up treasure for himself, and is not rich toward God" (Luke 12:16-21).

Jesus said in the above passage that he who gathers for himself is not rich toward God. God gives us possessions for the advancement of the kingdom. Whenever God blesses a believer, it is because He has the kingdom on his mind. However, what the spirit of Gehazi does is to redirect the treasure to building your own ego.

CHAPTER 9
Consequences of Greed

In the story of Gehazi, we see the specific sin of greed (and its accompanying vices of covetousness and materialism) and the way it destroyed the ministry of a man and his capacity to serve the Lord. The Bible warns us in so many places about the dangerous virus of greed, and it highlights the numerous consequences of greed's insidious attack.

1. It disqualifies you for the anointing.

Then he said to him, "Did not my heart go with you when the man turned back from his chariot to meet you? Is it time to receive money and to receive clothing, olive groves and vineyards, sheep and oxen, male and female servants? Therefore, the leprosy of Naaman shall cling to you and your descendants forever. And he went out from his presence leprous, as white as snow (2 Kings 5:26-27).

Gehazi was the servant of Elisha. He was his personal assistant and next in line for the anointing. The anointing comes by serving and serving well. Elisha had received a double portion because he had served Elijah well and was in the position to take the anointing to the next generation. Clearly, Gehazi was next in line for the anointing because it was trans-generational. The Bible makes it clear that when Elisha died, they took a dead man and put him in the same location as Elisha. After his bones touched Elisha's, the dead man came back alive. This is a proof that Elisha took the anointing with him because greed had disqualified Gehazi.

It's sad to see the end of a servant who had everything working for him and suddenly lost it because of greed. Gehazi broke a principle listed in the Old Testament because he went after the gifts from Naaman the leper. When a person was leprous, everything he touched, including garments became impure. By following Naaman and receiving gifts from him, Gehazi associated himself with the curse. Numerous people in the church and other ministries disqualify themselves from the anointing because they touch things or money they were not supposed to touch. Usually, the motivating factor is greed, and the cover-up involves ministry or church needs.

2. **It births lies.**

But Gehazi, the servant of Elisha the man of God, said, "Look, my master has spared Naaman this Syrian, while not receiving from his hands what he brought; but as the LORD lives, I will run after him and take something from him." So Gehazi pursued Naaman. When Naaman saw him running after him, he got down from the chariot to meet him, and said, "Is all well?"

Four Viruses Weakening The Church

And he said, "All is well. My master has sent me, saying, 'Indeed, just now two young men of the sons of the prophets have come to me from the mountains of Ephraim. Please give them a talent of silver and two changes of garments.'"

So Naaman said, "Please, take two talents." And he urged him, and bound two talents of silver in two bags, with two changes of garments, and handed them to two of his servants; and they carried them on ahead of him. When he came to the citadel, he took them from their hand, and stored them away in the house; then he let the men go, and they departed. Now he went in and stood before his master. Elisha said to him, "Where did you go, Gehazi?" And he said, "Your servant did not go anywhere" (2 Kings 5:22-25).

In Israel, there was a law forbidding the people to touch anything that was unclean, and leprosy was considered such. That's why the prophet Elisha did not accept anything from Naaman. Elisha had need in his ministry: he was leading a school of prophets, and the Bible even makes reference to a widow who had been married to one of those prophets and was now facing debt collectors because her husband had died broke. He was dealing with situations that needed financial intervention and resources. Please understand that I am not against financial support for ministries; we need money to do that which God has called us to do. But it's dangerous when we begin to compromise our message and mandate in order to secure financial support. A few years into my ministry, I learned that not every offer of money should be touched. You should not follow every connection that comes your way. Whatever you do, let it be under the guidance of the spirit of God and according to divine protocol. No amount of money can buy the anointing of God on your life.

Lies and greed are always best friends. They work in tandem. Whenever a person is greedy, it is easy for them to lie as well. When Elisha asked Gehazi a question about his whereabouts, Gehazi quickly began to lie.

3. It is a hindrance to practicing the Word.

As for you, son of man, your people who talk of you by the walls and in the doors of the houses say one to another, everyone to his brother, Come and hear what the word is that comes forth from the Lord.
And they come to you as people come, and they sit before you as My people, and they hear the words you say, but they will not do them; for with their mouths they show much love, but their hearts go after and are set on their [idolatrous greed for] gain.

Behold, you are to them as a very lovely [love] song of one who has a pleasant voice and can play well on an instrument, for they hear your words but do not do them (Ezekiel 33: 30-32 AMP).

In this passage, God is giving a clear idea of some types of churchgoers. They like coming to church, and they even go as far as inviting their siblings to come and hear the Word of Lord. However, in their hearts, the purpose of doing so is motivated by greed and the desire for gain. Many people bend the rules of God because they are motivated by greed. People lie and make crooked business deals because of the love of money. It's not the blessing that impresses, but it's the process that leads you to that blessing that is invaluable. The enemy can also bless but it's only the blessing of The Lord that makes rich and add no sorrow.

4. It results in a lack of sound judgment.

When a man is motivated by greed, he lacks the ability to make healthy decisions. The person is so possessed with greed and self-interest that he finds it easy to steal, lie and even kill as long as he gets what his heart desires.

And he told them this parable: "The ground of a certain rich man yielded an abundant harvest. He thought to himself, 'What shall I do? I have no place to store my crops.'

"Then he said, 'This is what I'll do. I will tear down my barns and build bigger ones, and there I will store my surplus grain. And I'll say to myself, "You have plenty of grain laid up for many years. Take life easy; eat, drink and be merry."'

"But God said to him, 'You fool! This very night your life will be demanded from you. Then who will get what you have prepared for yourself?'

"This is how it will be with whoever stores up things for themselves but is not rich toward God" (Luke 12:16-21 NIV).

The parable of the man who built a barn to store all his crops is a clear example of the lack of judgment of someone who is motivated by greed. How can you save crops for a lifetime without their perishing? He was unable to make a sound and proper judgment because greed was his motivation. We cannot allow greed to be the motivating factor of our decision making because it will cause us to hurt people, break relationships, and destroy lives.

5. It causes us to despise the blessing we already have.

One of the challenges of our time is learning to be content with where we are in God and in the process that His taking us through. *Hebrews 13:5 says, "Keep your lives free from the love of money and be content with what you have, because God has said, 'Never will I leave you; never will I forsake you.'"*

We have become greedy to the point that we easily become dissatisfied with what we have. Envy causes us to want what others have. We have to reset the priorities in our lives and rediscover the essence of life.

6. It births false teaching.

The Bible talks about false teachers who use the needs and weaknesses of the people to exploit them. *2 Peter 2:3 says, "In their greed, they will exploit you with false words" (ESV)*. Unfortunately, many have used the gospel as their quick way of getting rich and accumulating fortunes.

People are suffering everywhere, desperate for solutions in their relationships, in their families, in their finances, and in other areas of their lives. The enemy has succeeded in sowing the seeds of greed in the hearts of false preachers who exploit the people of God in order to frustrate and slow the work of the ministry and bring reproach to the work of God. Numerous false doctrines are born out of greed. Preachers are preying on the desperation of God's people who hunger to be ministered to. These false teachers invent vain prophesies to seduce people and to attract finances.

The Virus of Jezebel
(Witchcraft)

CHAPTER 10
What Is the Virus of Jezebel?

This spirit is the virus of witchcraft, manipulation and rebellion. It is one of the most common spirits in operation today. Even though this spirit is named after a woman, the reality is that whether you are a woman or a man, you can be the victim of this spirit. The name Jezebel means "Baal exulted," and it is no wonder that she was seeking after position and power. Jezebel was the daughter of Ethbaal, the king of the Sidonians, and wife of King Ahab of Israel (1 Kings 16:31). Jezebel has gone down in Bible history as the very worst example of evil. But we have to understand that the spirit behind Jezebel has been in operation since the beginning of time in the Garden of Eden when satan tempted Eve. The reason why this spirit is associated with Jezebel is that she yielded herself to this spirit and became an embodiment of it.

One of the reasons why this spirit is the most manifest in the end times is that the nature of this spirit is to counterfeit the power of God and lead God's people astray through manipulation. God's response to the spirit of Jezebel is the spirit of Elijah. The spirit of Elijah is dispatched to counter every activity of the spirit of Jezebel.

Behold, I will send you Elijah the prophet

Four Viruses Weakening The Church

Before the coming of the great and dreadful day of the LORD.

And he will turn the hearts of the fathers to the children,

And the hearts of the children to their fathers,

Lest I come and strike the earth with a curse.

(Malachi 4:5-6).

Wherever there is an Elijah, there will be a Jezebel; I'll show it to you as we continue our journey.

CHAPTER 11

Manifestation of the Virus of Jezebel

Many of us, at some point in our lives, have dealt with the spirit of Jezebel without even knowing it. It's crucial that we come to a higher level of spiritual detection concerning the devices of the enemy, so let's look at the different attributes of this vicious end time spirit.

1. Controlling Tactics

This attribute of the spirit of Jezebel is perhaps the most manifest in our society. People have left jobs, relationships, and even churches because of the controlling powers of the spirit of Jezebel. This virus shows in the forms of excessive control. They are three categories of people that the spirit of control looks for.

- **Hurts and wounded people**

People who are hurt and wounded in life often fall victim to the spirit of Jezebel. Ahab was hurt and emotional wounded when Naboth refused to sell his vineyard to him. That's when Jezebel asked him a question why are so hurt and wounded and she took advantage of a wounded king to insert her control in the situation. We must allow the Word of God to heal our wounds and hurts.

1 Kings 21:4-7

"⁴ So Ahab went into his house sullen and displeased because of the word which Naboth the Jezreelite had spoken to him; for he had said, "I will not give you the inheritance of my fathers." And he lay down on his bed, and turned away his face, and would eat no food. ⁵ But Jezebel his wife came to him, and said to him, "Why is your spirit so sullen that you eat no food?"

⁶ He said to her, "Because I spoke to Naboth the Jezreelite, and said to him, 'Give me your vineyard for money; or else, if it pleases you, I will give you another vineyard for it.' And he answered, 'I will not give you my vineyard.'"

⁷ Then Jezebel his wife said to him, "You now exercise authority over Israel! Arise, eat food, and let your heart be cheerful; I will give you the vineyard of Naboth the Jezreelite."

- **Naïve people**

The English dictionary describes a naive person as one who lacks experience, wisdom, or judgment. The spirit of Jezebel usually searches for these types of people in order to exercise its influence on them.

"The prudent sees the evil and hides himself, But the naive go on, and are punished for it" (Proverbs 22:3 NASB).

In Proverbs 9:4 The woman was specifically targeting those that are naïve in order to invite them in and commit fornication.

"Whoever is naive, let him turn in here!" To him who lacks understanding she says, Proverbs 9:4

Most of the time, the naïve person has a tendency to be too ready to believe someone or something or to trust that someone's intentions are good without deeper discernment. We cannot be naïve in life. Spiritual people should discern everything.

1 Corinthians 2:15 "But he that is spiritual judgeth all things, yet he himself is judged of no man.

- **Ignorant people**

To be ignorant simply means to lack knowledge or information. The bible says that without knowledge, my people perish. The spirit of control always looks for people that are ignorant of his agenda and works.

Hosea 4:6 "My people are destroyed for lack of knowledge; because you have rejected knowledge

Four Viruses Weakening The Church

When you are ignorant of God's word and the principle of prayers. When you are ignorant of the devices of the enemy. You are becoming a target for this virus to control you.

1 Timothy 3:13 Who was before a blasphemer, and a persecutor, and injurious: but I obtained mercy, because I did it ignorantly in unbelief.

Here are a few points that can help you discern if this spirit of Jezebel is trying to control your life.

- Are you feeling drain emotionally by someone or a situation in your life?
- Do you feel isolate from the people that can help you and influence your life?
- Are you feeling a sense of unhappiness, doubt, insecurity, and loss of spirituality?
- Are you pressured compromise your values to try to please another person?

2. **Manipulating Spirits**

The manipulation of Jezebel is often disguised, and most would believe that the witchcraft that is being exercised is actually the power of God in action. I believe in signs and wonders, but I have a problem with those who perform signs and wonders without having a prayer life or those who do the work of God without being consecrated. The works of the spirit of Jezebel are questionable, and it's just a matter of time before they are revealed. There is a difference between the signs and wonders performed by the Holy Ghost through faith and those that are performed by witchcraft.

Remember the story of Moses when he was in conflict with the magicians in Egypt:

Then the LORD spoke to Moses and Aaron, saying, "When Pharaoh speaks to you, saying, 'Show a miracle for yourselves,' then you shall say to Aaron, 'Take your rod and cast it before Pharaoh, and let it become a serpent.'" So Moses and Aaron went in to Pharaoh, and they did so, just as the LORD commanded. And Aaron cast down his rod before Pharaoh and before his servants, and it became a serpent.

But Pharaoh also called the wise men and the sorcerers; so the magicians of Egypt, they also did in like manner with their enchantments. For every man threw down his rod, and they became serpents. But Aaron's rod swallowed up their rods. And Pharaoh's heart grew hard, and he did not heed them, as the LORD had said.

So the LORD said to Moses: "Pharaoh's heart is hard; he refuses to let the people go.

Four Viruses Weakening The Church

Go to Pharaoh in the morning, when he goes out to the water, and you shall stand by the river's bank to meet him; and the rod which was turned to a serpent you shall take in your hand. And you shall say to him, 'The LORD God of the Hebrews has sent me to you, saying, "Let My people go, that they may serve Me in the wilderness"; but indeed, until now you would not hear! Thus says the LORD: "By this you shall know that I am the LORD. Behold, I will strike the waters which are in the river with the rod that is in my hand, and they shall be turned to blood. And the fish that are in the river shall die, the river shall stink, and the Egyptians will loathe to drink the water of the river."'"

Then the LORD spoke to Moses, "Say to Aaron, 'Take your rod and stretch out your hand over the waters of Egypt, over their streams, over their rivers, over their ponds, and over all their pools of water, that they may become blood. And there shall be blood throughout all the land of Egypt, both in buckets of wood and pitchers of stone.

And Moses and Aaron did so, just as the LORD commanded. So he lifted up the rod and struck the waters that were in the river, in the sight of Pharaoh and in the sight of his servants. And all the waters that were in the river were turned to blood. The fish that were in the river died, the river stank, and the Egyptians could not drink the water of the river. So there was blood throughout all the land of Egypt.

Then the magicians of Egypt did so with their enchantments; and Pharaoh's heart grew hard, and he did not heed them, as the LORD had said. And Pharaoh turned and went into his house. Neither was his heart moved by this. So all the Egyptians dug all around the river for water to drink, because they could not drink the water of the river. And seven days passed after the LORD had struck the river (Exodus 7:8-25).

I call this a counterfeit anointing. More frequently in our churches, we are seeing strange fire and a phony anointing. I have heard strange stories lately of so-called pastors who are using all kind of tricks to prophesy or perform miracles in order to manipulate the people of God. We need to come out of the spirit of carnality to be able to discern the operation of the spirit of Jezebel in our churches. However, the devil will never be able to copy some things because our God is in a class all by Himself. When the finger of God begins to move, even the magicians and witches will bow and acknowledge the great power of God.

Let me show you few indicators of a manipulative atmosphere:

- **Unquestioning submission**

A true Biblical submission always involves the full use of a person's will. Nobody can force you to submit. It's out of your own will that submission is born.
The biblical submission is done out of God's reverence and not man's fear.

Ephesians 5:21 submitting to one another in the fear of God.

- **Lack of accountability**

When you are in an atmosphere where people in leadership or place of authority are not accountable in anyone. The spirit of manipulation is easily at work.

- **Blaming others**

Often times, the people who blame others also have tendency to portray themselves as victims in order to manipulate a situation or circumstance.

- **Isolation**

Isolation is one of the main strategy of manipulation. Often times, the spirit of manipulation will try to isolate you from the people that you love and those that can help you. It makes feel that everybody is wrong or against you in order to have control and manipulate your feelings and emotions.

CHAPTER 12
Jezebel's Mission

1. Kill the heirs

When Athaliah the mother of Ahaziah saw that her son was dead, she arose and destroyed all the royal heirs. But Jehosheba, the daughter of King Joram, sister of Ahaziah, took Joash the son of Ahaziah, and stole him away from among the king's sons who were being murdered; and they hid him and his nurse in the bedroom, from Athaliah, so that he was not killed. So he was hidden with her in the house of the LORD for six years, while Athaliah reigned over the land (2 Kings 11:1-3).

Jezebel was married to Ahab, who was the king of Israel in the north before her daughter, Athaliah, married Jehoram, the king of Judah in the south. If you study your Bible carefully, you will realize that God had promised a Redeemer out of Judah. Jesus Christ was promised to come out of the seed of Judah.

Jehoram, a descendant of King David, actively promoted the worship of the Hebrew Lord in his country, but he tolerated Athaliah's worship of Baal. After Jehoram's death, their son Ahaziah became Judah's king with Athaliah acting as a regent queen mother. She used her power in that role to establish the worship of Baal in Judah after Ahaziah was killed in a state visit to Israel along with the then king of Israel, also named Jehoram, who was Athaliah's brother. Jehu assassinated both Ahaziah and Jehoram in Yahweh's name and had Athaliah's entire extended family in Israel murdered.

In Revelation 12, the Bible speaks of a great dragon waiting on a woman to give birth to a male child. Why was the dragon in waiting position? Because that child was to be a son of promise. He would be born with a mission and a mandate to fulfill.

Athaliah, as queen of Judah, had all possible heirs to the throne executed—except one. One of her grandsons, named Jehoash, was rescued from the purge by Jehosheba, Ahaziah's sister, and was raised in secret by the priest Jehoiada. Six years later, Athaliah was surprised when Jehoiada revealed Jehoash and proclaimed him king of Judah. She rushed to stop this rebellion but was captured and executed.

The spirit of Jezebel is still trying to kill ministries and ministers in their infancy stages so it can control and manipulate the church. However, I pray that God will raise up people like Jehosheba in our churches who can preserve the seed in the house of God through prayer and the nurturing of the Word until the seed is mature enough to follow God's mission and mandate.

Four Viruses Weakening The Church
2. Silencing the Prophetic Voice

.But when Herod's birthday was celebrated, the daughter of Herodias danced before them and pleased Herod. Therefore, he promised with an oath to give her whatever she might ask.
So she, having been prompted by her mother, said, "Give me John the Baptist's head here on a platter."
And the king was sorry; nevertheless, because of the oaths and because of those who sat with him, he commanded it to be given to her. So he sent and had John beheaded in prison. And his head was brought on a platter and given to the girl, and she brought it to her mother. Then his disciples came and took away the body and buried it, and went and told Jesus (Matthew 14:6-12).

When King Herod took his brother's wife to be his wife, John the Baptist spoke up against it. Because he had exposed the wickedness of the king, John the Baptist was put in prison. But Herod's new queen, his Brother Phillip's former wife, was operating under the spirit of Jezebel. When her daughter danced and it pleased the king, she was offered the privilege of choosing a gift. Among the thousands of gifts that her mother could have suggested, she told her daughter to choose the head of John the Baptist.

The spirit of Jezebel doesn't want to be uncovered. She wants to work in the background and advance her evil agenda. Whenever there is a true prophetic voice, the mask of Jezebel will be uncovered and her scheme exposed. The first thing the spirit of Jezebel seeks is the destruction of a true prophetic voice. Remember that Jezebel also has prophets that she's trying to introduce as legitimate. The spirit is of Jezebel doesn't like any confrontation because it operates by intimidating people and placing them under what I called a mind prison. It takes a person full of the Holy Ghost and boldness to confront her. If you notice this spirit in your life, family, marriage, or church and you don't confront it, you are giving her ground for operation.

Sometimes, we don't like to confront such a spirit because we want to keep peace in our domain. But believe me, as long as there is a Jezebel in your life, there is no way for you to experience the true peace of God. We must refuse to settle for imitation peace because of our fears. As long as there is a Jezebel, there will never be peace. Because Jezebel is a spirit that likes to operate covertly, she will be exposed whenever she is confronted.

3. Promote Idolatry

Jezebel is the carnal spirit that prophesies and teaches in the church system and seduces many to commit fornication.

Four Viruses Weakening The Church

"Notwithstanding I have a few things against thee, because thou sufferest that woman Jezebel, which calleth herself a prophetess, to teach and to seduce my servants to commit fornication, and to eat things sacrificed unto idols" (Revelation 2:20 KJV).

You have to understand that in this passage, fornication is not restricted to only the sexual act, but every time we associate ourselves with things that are not Christ-like, we commit fornication before God. We are in a covenant with God. The church is the bride of Christ, purchased by His precious blood. Whenever we begin to worship other gods or other things in our lives, we are committing spiritual fornication. Some Christians are married to the world and have, therefore, committed fornication before God. We are Christ's bride, called to be holy and spotless, faithful to our Lord and Savior. This spirit is behind all of the false worship that is deceiving God's people in all of the nations of our world. We are obligated to get rid of idolatry in our churches and to return to the true worship of God.

4. Bring Confusion

"And Elijah came to all the people, and said, 'How long will you falter between two opinions? If the LORD is God, follow Him; but if Baal, follow him.' But the people answered him not a word." (1 Kings 18:21).

The reason why the people of Israel did not answer Elijah is that they were confused. They didn't know whom to believe because lies had been rehearsed to them for so long.

Jezebel's virus is a counterfeit spirit which leaves people confused and uses their confusion to her advantage. Baal was believed to be the god of agriculture, and he also represented abundance and increase. As the queen in Israel, Jezebel influenced the people to worship Baal and persuaded them that Baal would grant them a harvest and increase. People began giving glory to idols and worshipping idols. God withheld the rain for three years to expose the powerlessness of Baal.

Many Christians have become confused in our churches. They no longer know what or who they should believe in. What is the truth and what are the lies of the Devil? We have lowered the standard for holiness and reduced the power of God to mere words, no longer preaching the gospel of repentance and transformation. As a consequence, people have become so carnal in our churches that they can no longer distinguish the spirit of Jezebel from the moving of God. I pray that every confusion sowed by the spirit of Jezebel in our churches, families, and lives will be destroyed by the light of the Word of God.

PART 5

Conclusion

Four Viruses Weakening The Church

CHAPTER 13
Cures

How can we overcome these viruses in our lives and churches so we can forcefully advance the kingdom of God and influence our generation for Christ? I'm grateful that God always provides a way for us to get back in line so we can experience His glory and power in our lives. In this chapter, I want to provide some simple steps to help you recover from the viruses and continue the work that He has entrusted to you.

1. **ACKNOWLEDGE**

The first step in the process of getting rid of a virus in our churches is to acknowledge the virus. We can never treat a sickness that we fail to identify and acknowledge. The same truth applies with every sin. When David was confronted with his sin, He had to acknowledge it before starting the process of repentance.

"I acknowledged my sin unto you, and my iniquity have I not hid. I said, I will confess my transgressions unto the LORD; and you forgave the iniquity of my sin" (Psalm 32:5).

When we acknowledge our sins as manifested in these viruses, we are taking responsibility.

Four Viruses Weakening The Church

Our God is a loving Father Who gave His Precious Son for His church. He wants to restore His church and his people, but all that He is waiting for from us is to admit where we have gone wrong. *"Only acknowledge your iniquity, that you have transgressed against the LORD your God, and have scattered your favors to the strangers under every green tree, and you have not obeyed my voice, says the LORD" (Jeremiah 3:13).* When we admit our sins to God, it's an indication that we are willing to change and return to Him.

2. REPENT

When anyone becomes aware that they are guilty in any of these matters, they must confess in what way they have sinned. Leviticus 5:5 (NIV)

The second power step is repentance. Repentance is a change of mind—when you ask God for forgiveness and make a decision to change the course of your actions. We all need to come to the altar of God and repent because of the viruses that we have allowed in our lives and churches. *"Repent, then, and turn to God, so that your sins may be wiped out, that times of refreshing may come from the Lord" (Acts 3:19 NIV).*

The season of refreshing comes when we are willing to repent. When we repent, God will send a restoration and a refreshment from the Holy Spirit in our lives.

3. BE SANCTIFIED

The best weapon again our Enemy is the life of sanctification and consecration.

When we clean our spirits of all works of flesh, the enemy does not have any tool to use against us. Jesus said the enemy has come against me but found none of his in me. John 14:30.

We need to clean our lives of any fleshly desires and seeds that can give the Enemy access in our lives. The key is sanctification. David said in *Psalm 51:10, "Create in me a clean heart, O God; and renew a right spirit within me."*

The first step to sanctification is to make Christ the Lord of your heart. Nothing that competes with God's Lordship in your heart should be allowed.

"In your hearts, set Christ as The Lord" (1 Peter 3:15b).

5. BE ACCOUNTABLE

The way of a fool is right in his own eyes, but a wise man is he who listens to counsel." Proverbs 12:15

As Christians, we need to learn to be accountable to one another for the benefit of the kingdom. Accountability is one of the means God uses to bring about solid growth and maturity with the freedom to be what God has created us to be. Accountability to others is simply one of the ways God holds us answerable to Him. Accountability helps us develop relationships with other Christians that help to promote spiritual reality, honesty, obedience to God, and genuine evaluation of our walk and relationship not only with God but also with others. Accountability brings about relationships that help the believer change by the Spirit of God and the truth of the Word of God through inward spiritual conviction and faith.

CHAPTER 14
Prayers for Repentance

Repent, then, and turn to God, so that your sins may be wiped out, that times of refreshing may come from the Lord" (Acts 3:19 NIV).

Father,

I come before your throne of our grace to ask for forgiveness for my sins. I repent of the ways that I have lived my life that didn't glorify Your holy name. I ask You today to create in me a clean heart and renew a right spirit within me. Let the meditation of my heart be acceptable before You. Let my life be a true reflection of Your glorious name.

Let my life be a living sacrifice holy and acceptable to You.

Let me always spread the perfume of Your love and compassion.

I close every door of pride, greed, deception, and fornication that has given access to the Enemy in my life.

I declare that I shall live for God and Him alone.

                                              Amen.

For Overcoming Greed

"For the love of money is the root of all evil: which while some coveted after, they have erred from the faith, and pierced themselves through with many sorrows"
(1 Timothy 6:10).

Four Viruses Weakening The Church

In the name of Jesus,

- I shall not be a victim of the spirit of Gehazi.
- I pray to be kept from the greed that would spoil my relationship with You.
- I'll seek God's face and not just ask for blessings from His hand.
- I will be faithful and content with God as my great reward.
- I'll not trade my spiritual inheritance for material gains.

For Overcoming Pride

My heart is not proud, O Lord, my eyes are not haughty; I do not concern myself with great matters or things too wonderful for me. But I have stilled and quieted my soul; like a weaned child with its mother, like a weaned child is my soul within me. O Israel, put your hope in the LORD both now and forevermore. Psalm 131

- I pray that every seed of arrogance in my life be uprooted.
- I renounced to proud look, attitude and expression.
- I bind every spirit of pride that is misleading my actions and decisions.
- I pray that I'll walk with the spirit of humility of the heart.

- I declare that I'll give God glory and honor for all the blessings in my life.
- I declare that I'll boast only in the Lord and The power of His salvation

For Overcoming Seduction

"For this is the will of God, [even] your sanctification, that ye should abstain from fornication: That every one of you should know how to possess his vessel in sanctification and honor" (I Thessalonians 4:3&4).

- I declare that every form of seduction in my life is destroyed.
- I shall not be a victim of the spirit of seduction.
- I declare that I shall walk in holiness and righteousness.
- I pray for restoration of marriages, families, churches, cities and communities in the name of Jesus.

For Overcoming Jezebel's spirit

"And you shall strike down the house of Ahab your master, so that I may avenge on Jezebel the blood of my servants the prophets, and the blood of all the servants of the Lord" (2 Kings 9:7).

Four Viruses Weakening The Church

- I take a stand to rebuke, bind, and banish every spirit of Jezebel in our churches, families, and communities.
- I war against this spirit's intimidation and control in order to set all captives free.
- I declare in faith that every chain on every captive that this spirit has is destroyed and broken.
- I break the power, manipulation, lies, denial, and deception caused by the spirit of Jezebel.
- I rebuke all spirits of false teaching & false prophecy in our churches.
- I bind up the powers of witchcraft through the blood of Jesus.
- I pray that all corruption, destruction, nakedness, and shame caused by Jezebel be exposed!
- I declare freedom, deliverance, healing, joy, and peace for all captives in the mighty name of Jesus.
- I claim this victory through the Blood of Jesus and by the Word of God.

CONTACT THE AUTHOR

Apostle Chris Fire has been travelling the globe bringing revival through crusades, conferences, teachings and mentoring.
Stay in touch with us:

CHRIS FIRE MINISTRIES
P.O BOX 6
Boyds MD 20841
www.Chrisfire.org
Phone: 240-232-6126

facebook.com/revivalrcm
Instagram.com/fire3chris
Tweeter.com/fire3chris
Periscope/fire3chris

www.ingramcontent.com/pod-product-compliance
Lightning Source LLC
Chambersburg PA
CBHW071308040426
42444CB00009B/1934